Monitoring: A Guide for Remote Viewing & Professional Intuitive Teams

Lori Lambert Williams

Learn the rare skill that few people truly understand: How to help remote viewers and professional intuitives as they work their way through a session.

Remote Viewers and Professional Intuitives have long needed a trustworthy partner to help them stay safe and obtain requested psychic information without leading them astray.

Now anyone can learn how to work in a dependable remote viewing team.

intuitivespecialists.com

ISBN: 978-0-9994289-1-7

Printed in the United States of America

Monitoring: A Guide for Remote Viewing & Professional Intuitive Teams
by Lori Williams
Cover Design: Michelle Ivanovich

First Edition, 2017

10 9 8 7 6 5 4 3 2 1

Acknowledgements

Whenever I buy a new book, I always read the acknowledgements. When I read all the names of people the author is thanking, I'm always surprised by how many people I know! If you are one of the people who actually read the acknowledgements page, thank you for being here! Maybe you will see someone you know among these pages.

My first acknowledgement must go to my husband, best friend, life companion, therapist, handyman, and world-class monitor, Jim Williams. I've never met anyone who can monitor better than you, my love! Remember the day we decided to give a joint monitoring class to my online Mentoring Club? That class formed the core of this book! Thank you, Sweetheart, for always being here for me and for the students. Without your suggestions, advice, opinions and support, this book would never have been written.

Additionally, I want to thank my Advanced Viewing Team: Pawel Trela, Jed Bendix, Moselle Bernal, Eileen Fitzpatrick, Patsy Posey, Bernard (Andy) Raum, Ed Wilde, Michael Ash, Sheila Dugan, Patricia Hung, Nathalie Bentolila, Joan Toebes, Calin Coltea, Ellen DiNucci, Chris Kempner and Nancy McBreen for being so supportive. Each one of you, your requests and questions have been the seeds that gave birth to this book. Thanks for your years of belief in me and your willingness to help.

Many thanks to my wonderful step-daughter, Gayle Williams for your editing, formatting and proof reading skills that allowed this book make it to print! Michelle Ivanovich, thank you for the time you spent in copyediting, proofing, and most of all, the gorgeous cover you designed for this book! You listened to my ideas, and when I saw the cover, I knew you had plucked it right out of my head! You are truly a master!

I'm so grateful to my parents—my father, Darrel Holt, whose love of language, books and an interest in the supernatural was passed on to me. My mother, Kathryn Holt, always believed I would write a book someday, and encouraged me that I could do anything. I love you, Mom!

Thanks to my children, Almond, Michael, Dustin, Keana, Mary, Joe, Megan, Gayle and Chris. You guys inspire me to do greater things! I love you all so much!

I'd like to thank Melvin Riley, who has provided me with many words of wisdom and comfort along my journey, helping me to maneuver through times of confusion and discouragement. Mel, thanks for being such a good CRV colleague. I am honored to call you a friend.

And a gratitude page would not be complete without expressing my greatest appreciation to my mentor, Lyn Buchanan. Lyn, the day I met you in 1996 changed my life forever. You have given me so much of your time, effort, and probably a lot of consternation over the years! I can never thank you enough.

Lastly, thank you to all my students from all over the world who have taken my courses, asked the questions, and done the work to learn the amazing skill of Controlled Remote Viewing. I believe in you! Now, with this tool, you will reach even greater heights. I used to say, "The sky is the limit." No more. There is no limit! Go for it!

Table of Contents

Foreword

Edgar Cayce, the famous "sleeping prophet," had one.

Barbara Marciniak, author of the famed channeling series that began with her best seller, *Bringers of the Dawn: Teachings from the Pleiadians,* had one.

In fact, the most famous seers, channelers, prophets and mystics throughout history were blessed with the assistance of unsung heroes. Who were these "unsung heroes?"

These were the people who tirelessly recorded everything that was said; the quiet helpers who made sure that all the little details were taken care of for the person whose job it was to share information from God, the Cosmos, or The Source.

What you are about to read is a guide that will provide you, the reader, with enough information that you can become "the keeper of the words" in a very real sense. What does this mean?

Remote Viewing is an ancient science—one that has been practiced for millennia. Yet, when the U.S. military became involved—needing a top-notch team of well-trained psychics to counteract the loss of intelligence to enemies in other countries—then "Remote Viewing" was suddenly no longer an ancient mystic art, lost in the dusty attic of history. Instead, it has become a buzz word that encompasses a wide array of telepathic and clairaudient phenomena allowing the skilled practitioner to access any information, anywhere in all of Time and Space.

In today's world, the mystic, seer and/or psychic is now called a "remote viewer." And the unsung hero? The one who supports the remote viewer and makes sure that he/she is in the best possible circumstances to receive accurate information? We call him or her "The Monitor."

What follows is information gleaned from many years of remote viewing experience and training. My name is Lori Williams. I became involved with remote viewing in 1996 after a lifetime of strange paranormal experiences for which I had no explanation. Fortunately, the Universe saw fit to have my path cross with that of Lyn Buchanan, a former military remote viewer. Lyn and his wife took me under their caring wings, becoming much like second parents to me.

Under Lyn's tutelage, I learned to remote view professionally, to teach remote viewing, and even how to run professional remote viewing projects. It goes without saying that along the way, I learned how to monitor and to be monitored. When I married Jim Williams in 2005, he was already trained as a remote viewer and had begun monitoring me professionally a few years before.

Jim became (and remains) a world-class monitor. Since learning how to monitor remote viewers trained in the method known as *Controlled Remote Viewing* or CRV, Jim has been flown to locations to monitor professional viewers on various targets, and has accompanied me all over the world to ensure I had the best of care while doing my job as a Viewer and as an Instructor of remote viewing.

While most of the references within this guide are attuned more to the Controlled Remote Viewer, they can (and should) be adapted for any professional who provides intuitive services. If you are a Controlled Remote Viewer (herein after referred to as a "CRV'er") and you have never had the pleasure of remote viewing with a trained Monitor, you are missing out on something major. You will find that your remote viewing skills will skyrocket when you have the benefit of viewing with a Monitor.

By the same token, if you are a professional intuitive, psychic, medium or channeler, you will find this guide to be of invaluable help to you. With this book, you will be able to train any reasonably quiet person to be the support you've needed and longed for.

As you read these pages, you are joining the ranks of many brave pioneers. Think of Columbus crossing the ocean to the new land! Think of the Apollo program, exploring the realms outside Earth's gravitational field! That is who we are. That is who YOU are. All of us—we are exploring the frontiers of ***Consciousness***. And that, my friend, is still very much uncharted territory.

Remember that we live in highly uncertain times... even dangerous times. Many of us consider Controlled Remote Viewing and Extended Remote Viewing to be "The Survival Tools of the Future."

I am honored to share this information with you. Good luck on your journey! And thank you for your willingness to help the Mystics of our current age.

Introduction

Things have changed somewhat since the days of the military's Stargate Remote Viewing Program. Thankfully, most of us don't have Generals watching us as we do dog-and-pony shows to demonstrate the efficacy of remote viewing. Rarely, if ever, do we have big crowds to control during a remote viewing session, and we don't have to view with electrodes attached to our heads for research.

Speaking with several of these original military remote viewers, I've heard them say more than once, "***A good Monitor is essential to a successful remote viewing session.***" Yet monitoring as a skill and as an important component to the remote viewing process has been seriously under-valued by contemporary civilian remote viewers.

The men in the military program often had the advantage of being physically present in one place, viewing and monitoring, usually in a team setting.

Today's remote viewers often find themselves viewing alone. Their targets are very diverse, coming from corporate, private, law enforcement, personal, scientific, archeological, esoteric, technological, and futuristic sources.

With the suggestions outlined below, it is our hope that you, the reader, will be able to use this manual to train a friend, a spouse, or even a mature teenager to monitor you.

Eventually, though, you will find yourself in a situation in which you have to view alone. The information presented here will also help you immensely as you *learn to monitor yourself.*

By faithfully practicing the suggestions within these pages, you will find that your conscious mind can be a tremendous asset to the Controlled Remote Viewing process.

How?

Your conscious mind becomes the interviewer.

Think about a reporter: a reporter must ask the who, what, when, where, why and how of any situation, right?

CRV is an interview-and-report methodology!

So, your subconscious mind has the information, and the conscious mind becomes the interviewer, asking all the right questions.

One fine morning, I woke up and realized that there is no written guide anywhere to show today's Remote Viewers the real nuts and bolts of the remote viewing *monitoring* process. "If having a good Monitor is crucial to the success of any session, "I thought, "having a complete 'How To' guide to *monitoring* is essential!" And here it is!

Many of my students look terrified the first time I ask them to monitor. "But, I don't know *how* to be a Monitor!" they plead. I reassure them that I will be there, guiding them through the whole process.

So, don't let the word "monitoring" scare you. Everything you need to know to get started is right here, in the pages that follow.

A lot of people think that monitoring a Remote Viewer is all about doing everything perfectly—

saying all the right things, and taking all the right actions at the right moment. That puts a lot of pressure on you as a Monitor, doesn't it?

Just remember this:

RV monitoring *isn't* about the *Monitor*.

RV monitoring *is* all about the *Viewer*.

Have you ever noticed how a lot of people don't know how to just *observe* and *tune in* to another person? It can be tough to do that, because most of us are living inside our own heads so much, and are often so busy thinking about ourselves:

"Am I doing it right?"

"What does he think of me?"

"I'm getting hungry. Is it time for lunch yet?"

Observing the Viewer and eventually becoming adept at literally *reading* the Viewer's body language and subtle emotional ups and downs is truly at the heart of good remote viewing monitoring.

Note: This manual is written for both the student Viewer and Monitor practicing together and for professional CRV teams. In practice situations, the Monitor is choosing the targets for the Viewer, and therefore has a lot of target information available as feedback. When doing professional remote viewing operations, the Monitor is working with a Project Manager, who is working directly with the customer or client. Depending on the situation, the Project Manager decides how much information about the target to share with the Monitor. He or she may decide not to share ***anything*** *about the target with the Monitor. That is called a "double blind" situation, because both Viewer and Monitor are blind to the target. In other scenarios, the Project Manager and Monitor consult with each other closely throughout the project in order to ensure that the Viewer obtains the needed information.*

How to Find a Monitor: CRV Buddies!

For the majority of Viewers today, no one is getting paid to view eight hours a day. Most Viewers are balancing career and family demands while finding time to explore this fascinating new path of consciousness!

When you know you need to exercise, it is much more motivating and fun to have someone to share your pain—a walking or gym partner, for example. You schedule a time to meet and exercise. Knowing that another person has committed time to work with you helps you get past the malaise and lethargy that thwarted your efforts in the past. You keep those appointments, because you don't want to let the other person down, right?

In the Intuitive Specialists' **Online Mentoring Club**, we've found that by forming "CRV Buddies" and having the students view and monitor each other, contemporary viewing skills are improving by leaps and bounds.

The benefits of working with a buddy:

- Viewers and Monitors get more practice time because they know they have someone waiting to work with them.
- The Viewers learn what they need to get the most information out of a target.
- The Monitors learn from the monitoring experience how to be better Viewers.
- Both Viewers and Monitors learn how to get curious about a target and how to ask and answer the right questions along the way.

This guide will address the needs of the individual Viewer, as well as today's Viewer-Monitor teams, who often work together online rather than face-to-face, coordinating convenient times to meet.

We aim to help both newcomers and experienced Viewer-Monitor teams avoid the most common pitfalls.

You'll learn the "tips of the pros" gained through years of experience!

And although this guide is geared toward the Controlled Remote Viewer, or CRV'er—much of the information can be adapted and used by psychics and professional intuitives. You should get plenty of ideas about how to get more detail, and come to understand how having a trained partner during your psychic work can help you become more versatile. If you happen to be a professional intuitive, a lot of the information you will find here can be adapted for the work you do.

I have even used some of the methods in this course in my former career as a hypnotist, as these tips help to avoid common pitfalls of "leading" and "polluting." We will discuss those terms later on.

The benefits of working as a team on any project or practice target cannot be emphasized enough.

If you do not currently have a CRV Buddy or someone to practice with regularly, we suggest you post your need for a remote viewing partner on one of the more reputable Facebook Remote Viewing pages or, if you are a member, on the

CRV Yahoo E-group List.

Note: In order to join the Yahoo CRV E-group, you must have graduated from a recognized Controlled Remote Viewing course taught by one of the following instructors: Lyn Buchanan, Lori Williams, Teresa Frisch, Paul O'Connor, or Paul Smith.

If you are one of our students, feel free to contact us so we can assist you.

Email: info@intuitivespecialists.com

The Monitor's Job

Choosing Practice Targets for the Viewer

When you get into operational, professional, or "real world" remote viewing, the Project Manager or Director will have agreed to take on a project from a customer or client. But for most new Viewer-Monitor teams, the Monitor will often be choosing the practice target for the Viewer.

Safety is the primary concern when choosing a target for a new Viewer. Choose a target that is safe and fun, interesting, has a lot of color, and has a variety of essential elements, such as land, water, manmade objects, people, animals, activities, or events.

Keep in mind that what you consider to be benign may not be benign for all Viewers. For example, you might pick a photo of a circus with a happy clown, not realizing that your Viewer has a clown phobia. Sometimes, you find out about a phobia only after you've assigned the target and the Viewer has reacted. But that's okay. Be familiar with how to detox effectively and assist the Viewer if needed, to ensure that the Viewer detoxes thoroughly. The Intuitive Specialists Viewer's Manual has more information about detoxing. There is also a chapter on detoxing in my upcoming book, *"Boundless: Your How-To Guide to Practical Remote Viewing!"*

Once a Viewer has gained experience through multiple practice sessions, you can practice with targets that are more involved, or that have aspects of moving through time (past, present, and future elements).

Be sure not to choose targets that are digitally or electronically manufactured or manipulated. We've all seen them. Remember the ads with a "photo" of a bunch of people smoking cigarettes while sitting on the wing of an airplane flying at 30,000 feet? That appears to be a terrific target, but it isn't *real.*

"Why does that matter?" you ask? Because Controlled Remote Viewers are trained to mentally go to the actual *target site*, not to the photo within the envelope. If that target site does not exist, the Viewer has nothing to view. So, choose targets wisely.

My website, **IntuitiveSpecialists.com** has a lot of good, benign targets for new Viewers. More experienced Viewers can find excellent targets for all levels of experience at Lyn Buchanan's website: www.crviewer.com. Look for the Target of the Week (TOTW) on Lyn's site.

Get to Know Your Viewer

As you start to work with a CRV Buddy on a regular basis, you will need to begin by using practice targets. We don't recommend trying to work "double blind" just yet. Using targets that you (as the Monitor) have chosen for the Viewer and are familiar with will allow you to get to know the Viewer's style of viewing and personal viewing habits.

By observing the Viewer and through your discussion with him/her afterwards, you can learn his/her preferences and expectations. Some Viewers prefer lots of verbal cueing and even some chitchat from the Monitor. Others prefer the Monitor to sit and not say anything.

One way to be sure that you learn all the nuances about your Viewer partner is to keep very good notes. Each time you sit down to monitor someone, have paper handy. We call these notes "The Monitor's Worksheet." (See Appendix C for the Monitor's Worksheet.)

The Monitor's Worksheet

The Monitor's worksheet is a wonderful tool that will allow any Monitor to start noticing patterns and micromovements that are particular to a certain Viewer. If you work with the same Viewer session after session, your Monitor's worksheets will soon be full of helpful information that will show you how your Viewer works.

That information will lead you to learn things about the target—especially later, when you and your Viewer will be working "real world" operational targets for real people, corporations, police, etc. You will be able to tell when the Viewer is on target, what information is really important, and when the Viewer is off target.

Below are some guidelines to help you understand what the Worksheet is for. You can even create your own!

The Monitor's Worksheet Guidelines

Each Monitor's Worksheet should contain:

1. The Viewer's name.
2. Viewer number (aka: V#) if he or she has one.
3. The Coordinate number you have assigned to the target.
4. A place to keep track of the session pages. (A Viewer can lose track of which page they are on once they are in a good remote viewing state.)
5. Note your name as the Monitor and list any observers who may be present to watch.
6. If any frontloading or information was given to the Viewer, be sure to write that down, word-for-word, exactly as it was given.
7. List the gestalts that the Viewer comes up with in Phase/Stage 1—and if any come up later during the session, write those down, too.
8. As the Viewer begins getting information, be sure to note any perceptions of interest

that you might want to move him or her to later.

9. Note the Viewer's micromovements. (For more information, see chapter entitled "What Are Micromovements?")
10. Note any reactions that the Viewer is having to you or to the target and be sure to include the page number of the session so you can refer to it later, in case you and the Viewer want to discuss what happened.

The Monitor's Worksheet

V #:	Viewer's Name:	Monitor's Name:

Date:	Target Coordinate:	Frontloading Given (if any):

Break Times:	Resume Times:	List Any Observers:	Gestalts to Cue From:

Track Page Numbers with Tic Marks Here:

Micromovements:	Perceptions to Explore Further:

Notes	Page #'s to Remember:

The Nuts and Bolts of the CRV Session

HOW TO SET UP

You and the Viewer should sit across from each other so you have an unobstructed view of the Viewer's face and hands.

Make sure everything is "just so"—the way the Viewer likes it. This may mean a lap desk with white paper, a black gel pen, and drinking water nearby. Both of you need to be comfortable. The lighting should be good enough to see.

(Note: People sometimes ask me if Viewers need to view in a "grey room" like the military guys did. No! The more visual distractions, the busier the conscious mind will be, fielding all the visual information coming in. That is a good thing! Let's keep that conscious mind busy and out of the way!)

Once the Viewer has done whatever it is that he or she prefers to do to begin a session (praying, meditating, listening to music, doing yoga, working out, or any other activity that helps them feel "ready" to view) it is time for the actual session to begin.

THE ADMIN SECTION

As things get started on a new session, the Viewer should be doing the Admin Section of the first page—listing his or her name, the date, the time, the Monitor's name, any observers, any hunches or ideas he or she has about the target, any issues that may bother or distract him/her during the session—and then he/she begins going through the three steps of the Set Aside process.

(If you have no idea what the "Set Aside process" is, you can read all about it at IntuitiveSpecialists.com in the Blog section. Look for: *How to Set Aside Anything and Get On With Your Life!*)

The right upper corner of Page 1 is where all of this gets written down. In case some of my readers are new at CRV, or in case you happen to be working with a professional intuitive (rather than someone trained in CRV) you will find all the information you need about this section of the session, known as *The Admin Section*, in Appendix D.

That quick list of what belongs in the Admin Section can give you some ideas of what to have the person you are working with write down on the first page.

WHAT HAPPENS NEXT

Once the Set Aside process is finished, the Monitor should **wait until the Viewer's hand moves to the left side of the page, *below* the last line that was written on the right.**

You may need to remind the Viewer to "keep moving down the page." We always move *down* the page, never back up. That way, anyone who looks at the session later (including you and the Viewer) will always know the *order* that things occurred, how the perceptions came in, etc. That can become important later when doing post-session analysis.

Wait until the Viewer's pen is touching the paper on the left side before saying anything more.

Why do you have to be sure that the Viewer's pen is touching the paper?

Remember that *the body is the link between conscious and subconscious minds.* If the Viewer's pen is not **touching** the paper, it means that on a subconscious level, he or she is not quite ready yet.

There have been times that I *thought* my pen was touching the paper, and I was waiting for Jim to give me the coordinates so I could begin the session.

"Are you going to give me the coordinates?" I ask.

"Yes, as soon as you are ready," he always responds.

As soon as the Viewer's pen is touching the paper, **the first question you will ask is, "Would you like frontloading?"**

Frontloading

Often the Viewer receives no information about the target prior to the viewing. However, we have found that it can be beneficial to give the Viewer some broad and neutral information beforehand, as it helps the Viewer become accustomed to pollution. This neutral information is known as *frontloading*. The decision as to whether any particular session is frontloaded beforehand is always the Viewer's. The Monitor is never to force the Viewer to accept frontloading.

The true purists of remote viewing feel that a Viewer should never be given any information about the target, regardless of how neutral. Over the many years I have been working with Viewers and doing sessions myself, I disagree. Here's why:

Real life happens. Someone accidentally gives the Viewer too much information. The Viewer who has never been given any frontloading will be unable to view under these circumstances.

Frontloading is a form of pollution—a very slight form of pollution. But pollution will occur every now and then, and if a Viewer never experiences it, he or she will be too darned delicate to be able to work past that pollution and do a good session.

Some Viewers like to practice doing both; in other words, they do some sessions with frontloading and some sessions without frontloading. I usually advise my students to alternate, using frontloading for every other practice session. For the practice sessions in between those with frontloading, the Viewer should view with nothing but the coordinates beforehand. This way, the Viewer is more versatile, and gains experience viewing both *with* and *without* frontloading.

The most important thing that you, Monitor, need to remember is that it is the Viewer's choice. If the Viewer chooses to receive frontloading from you, **be sure any frontloading is completely neutral and non-leading.** Use the examples below to help you learn how to formulate good frontloading.

A Few Examples of Neutral Frontloading:

The Target is manmade. Describe the Target.
The Target is a location. Describe the Target.
The Target is biological. Describe the Target.
The Target is an activity. Describe the Target.
The Target is a person. Describe the Target.

Examples of Advanced Frontloading:

(The following examples are less common, and should only be given to very experienced, seasoned Viewers)

The Target is a Journey. Describe the Target.
The Target is a Process. Describe the Target.
The Target is a Life Path. Describe the Target.
The Target is a Technology. Describe the Target.
The Target is a Society. Describe the Target.

What to Look for in Every Remote Viewing Session

Observe the Viewer, and pay special attention to:

- **Voice**—Are there changes in the Viewer's tone, pitch or volume?
- **Posture**—What is the Viewer's body saying?
- **Eye movements**—Where is the Viewer looking?
- **Handwriting**—The Viewer's handwriting often changes dramatically and can become illegible due to the shift from left-brain to right-brain function.
- **Spelling**—Spelling is also a left-brain function, so spelling ability usually deteriorates as the Viewer gets immersed in the target.
  (Misspelled words can contain information about the target!)
- **Gestures or Ticks**—Certain gestures, nervousness or emotional demonstrations

can signal a reaction to the target site. As a Monitor, you will have to be aware of even the slightest reaction on the Viewer's part because over time, patterns of micromovements and other indicators will become evident. This will help you, if you ever find that you must take off your Monitor's hat and put on your Project Manager's hat, to know what to include and what not to include in the Project Report to the customer.

- **Micromovements**—Be sure to study the Viewer's micromovements. Learn to respond to them in a way that will not be noticeable to the Viewer. Keep dependable notes. This can become very crucial information when working an operational target.

The Viewer is Always Right

If the Viewer becomes irritable or angry, or lashes out at the Monitor, the Monitor should simply apologize, and discreetly make a note of what happened on the Monitor's Worksheet, including the page number of the session. This way both the Monitor and the Viewer can refer to that page of the session later, to see what was going on. This discussion should never be done during the viewing. Wait until the session is over to bring it up and discuss it. Why?

If an argument ensues during the viewing, it will destroy the session! A good Monitor knows that the Viewer is very vulnerable during a remote viewing session, and can be reacting to the target. Don't take anything personally! Simply make a note on your worksheet about the incident. Be sure to do this quietly. Remember, *it's not about you.*

After the session is over, the Monitor and Viewer may want to discuss what happened to see if the uncharacteristic outburst was caused by something at the target site that the Viewer was reacting to.

If you are new to remote viewing, you may wonder, "Why would a Viewer be reacting to something at the target site?" There are the obvious reasons, such as if someone unwisely gave the Viewer a target containing violence, horror, or death. But a Viewer can react to a target simply because something at the target site reminds the Viewer of something unpleasant in his or her past.

Since a lot of what is going on with the Viewer is below his or her conscious awareness, the subsequent reaction can bubble to the surface, manifesting as an emotional outburst or irritation towards the Monitor, extraneous noises, etc.

Keeping this in mind will help the Monitor not take anything personally.

What are Micromovements?

Remember that the body is the link between the conscious and subconscious minds. As the Viewer gets good site contact with the chosen target, you will begin to notice certain inflections in the voice, sighs, far off looks, body gestures, and other indicators that are manifested by way of the Viewer's physical body.

When these become dependable indicators—meaning that the Viewer unconsciously gives a certain indicator, such as pulling on an ear when on target or perhaps licking his or her lips when off target—you have begun to learn the Viewer's "micromovements."

Micromovements are subtle "tells" (like in a poker game) that the Viewer's subconscious mind creates in his or her own movements. The Viewer is not aware of these micromovements. Be sure *not* to tell the Viewer about his or her micromovements! Once the Viewer is made aware of their micromovements, these movements are no longer subconscious—they are now conscious. So, keep them to yourself. You will see why this is so important as you keep reading.

A Monitor who works with a Viewer on a regular basis can begin to read these movements and gain understanding from them. When the Monitor has chosen the target for the Viewer, the Monitor knows exactly when the Viewer is on target and when he or she is off.

Let's use Viewer "Lori" and Monitor "Jim" as an example. (Notice how I didn't change the names to protect the innocent?)

As Lori gets *on* target, she suddenly tips her head to the left. Jim notes it and subtly scratches his nose on purpose. Jim's nose scratching lets Lori's *subconscious* mind know that her Monitor, Jim, noticed the head-tipping signal. Meanwhile, consciously, Lori has *no* idea that any of this subconscious conversation is occurring.

When Lori gets *off* target, she may sigh heavily. Jim can once again *consciously choose* to make a gesture, such as rubbing his arm, to signal to

Lori's subconscious mind that he noticed the sigh. It is almost as though Jim is giving a subtle "thank you" to Lori's subconscious mind.

Micromovements become a conversation between the Monitor's ***conscious*** mind and the Viewer's ***sub***conscious mind. If the same Viewer-Monitor team practices regularly, this conversation can become a very dependable way for the Monitor to know when the Viewer is on or off target.

This is crucial when the team is working an operational, or "real world," target. When working on real, non-practice targets, neither the Viewer nor the Monitor knows what the target or answer is, but the Monitor who has studied his or her Viewer carefully will know when the Viewer's information is the most accurate or inaccurate based on the Viewer's micromovements.

Again, this is why it is extremely important for the monitor to know what the target is during practice sessions, as it allows the monitor to learn the Viewer's micromovements.

Jim and I have been working together as a remote viewing team since 2004. As a result, Jim is very familiar with my micromovements. Because of that, if I were asked by the police to view the location of a missing child, for example, Jim is able to note the parts of my session in which I am providing accurate information based on his observations of my micromovements. He can then make sure to include that information in his Project Report to the police.

The better you know your Viewer—including quirks, personality, and habits—the easier it becomes to know when the Viewer is or isn't on target.

Obviously, learning the Viewer's micromovements means *paying attention.* Just how observant does a Monitor have to be? VERY observant. And equally obvious is the fact that, working alone, you can't really learn about ***your own*** micromovements. As I mentioned above, they are subconscious, meaning that they are below your awareness. That's OK. You can still use a lot of this information to observe yourself. The following list can be a great reference tool for any Monitor—even when you are the Viewer, monitoring yourself.

Take Care of the Viewer

When you notice the Viewer reacting to something, you may not know at first what is happening. Ask yourself: What does the Viewer need?

- A cue to move to another part of the site?
- A break?
- Something to eat or drink?

It can be helpful to take a break to discuss what is happening.

Let the Viewer guide you, and be sensitive to the Viewer's needs.

It can be very irritating for a Viewer if the Monitor is too quick to try to help, so it is imperative for the Monitor to pay attention to subtle ways the Viewer may indicate a need for a cue. You can always ask a gentle question to clarify what the Viewer needs from you right then. The answer may be: "Sit there and shut up."

Some suggestions of a question to gently ask the Viewer are:

- Are you okay?
- What is happening?
- How do you feel?
- Do you need to stop and rest?

Don't ask more than one question at a time!

Again, pay attention to the Viewer's subtle indicators.

Cueing

One reason a Monitor is such a valuable part of the remote viewing team is because there can be moments during a remote viewing session in which the Viewer comes to a dead halt, unsure of where to go next.

When this happens, the Monitor can offer a gentle prod to the Viewer's subconscious mind through a process called "***Cueing***."

First, let's talk about "***Cues***."

Cues are generic, non-leading words used by the Monitor to prompt the Viewer for more information about the target.

When cues can be given:

- If the Viewer seems to be "stuck" or has drawn a blank and stopped viewing.
- When the Viewer has moved to a new part of the target site.
- To help the Viewer interact with the target.

Always remember that the Viewer is in charge of the session! So, don't be pushy. Let the Viewer guide you, and be sensitive to the Viewer's needs.

It can be irritating for a Viewer if the Monitor is too quick to cue.

If you feel it is a good time to give a cue, gently ask, "Would you like a cue?"

If the Viewer has just moved to a new part of the target, you may quietly offer some one-word cues.

One-Word Cues

One-word cues include words that prompt the Viewer for descriptors. When the Viewer has just moved into Phase/Stage 2, for example, the Monitor can quietly and quickly cue with "Colors? Smells? Sounds? Tastes? Textures? Luminance? Ambience?" These are examples. Check your Cue Card at the end of this chapter for more suggestions.

Wait until the Viewer has gotten dimensional perceptions before moving on to dimensional cues. Once the Viewer has gotten perceptions that describe the shape or size or pattern of something, the Monitor can add cues such as "Shapes? Sizes? Patterns? Positions? Measures?" Again, these are just examples. Your Cue Card has more dimensional hints.

After the Viewer has moved to a new part of the target, it's a good time for the Monitor to give some of the one-word cues mentioned above.

One-word cues should be given gently, in a quiet voice, and in quick succession, so that the Viewer cannot answer each cue. These one-word cues are meant to be a prod to the

subconscious mind, not questions. If the Monitor says "Color?" and the Viewer responds with "Red," the Viewer may be conjuring up answers just to please the Monitor. So read or say the cueing words very quickly.

Movement Commands and Action Cues

A Movement Command is a cue designed to help the Viewer move to another part of the target site. Examples include: "Move to the manmade and describe" or "Move 50 feet above the target and describe what you see."

A movement command should only be given if the Viewer indicates they would like to move somewhere else, or appears stuck. The Monitor can also use movement commands to guide the Viewer closer to something needed. For example, the target is a Ferris wheel. The Viewer already found "circular" and "rotating." The Monitor can suggest, "Move to the 'rotating' and describe," allowing the Viewer to move closer to the Ferris wheel.

Movement commands always begin with the magic word: "Move." When a movement command is given, *the Viewer must always stop viewing and write the entire cue down, word for word, across the page of the session transcript.* (Remember that the Viewer is in charge of the session. If the Viewer refuses, that could indicate that the Monitor interjected a movement command when the Viewer wasn't ready.)

The reason for writing down the movement command into the session transcript is so that later, when someone is examining the session, it will be easy to see where and when the Viewer moved around the target. The perceptions gathered after each movement command will be understood as pertaining to the part of the target the Viewer moved to, rather than something else.

An Action Cue helps the Viewer interact with the target. Examples include "Mentally lick the target. Taste?" or "Mentally slap the target. Density?" When an action cue is given, there is no need for the Viewer to write the cue down, because the Viewer is not moving to another part of the target. The Viewer is simply interacting with the target right where they are, and the resulting perceptions will simply get written down as a part of the descriptions he or she is perceiving.

Notice how each movement command or action cue is in two parts: The first part is a command to the Viewer's subconscious mind. The second part is a cue to the Viewer's conscious mind. We

need to give that conscious mind something to do! Let's keep it busy and out of the way!

The Monitor's Cue Card:

Below is the Cue Card with examples to help you come up with creative ideas for cueing your Viewer. Create your own to fit your needs and keep it handy when you are monitoring.

SENSORY WORDS:	DIMENSIONAL WORDS:
Colors? Illumination? Textures? Density? Temperature? Smells? Tastes? Sounds? Ambience?	Shapes? Sizes? Patterns? Positions? Direction? Orientation?
ACTION CUE EXAMPLES:	**MOVEMENT COMMAND EXAMPLES:**
Mentally lick the target. Taste? Mentally slap the target. Density? Clap your hands at the target. Sounds?	Move 10 feet back from the target and describe. Move 50 feet above the target and describe. Move 2 minutes forward and describe. Move underneath the target and describe. Move 12 hours forward and describe what you see. Turn 180° degrees at the target and describe.
OCCASIONAL QUESTIONS:	**ADVANCED CUES:**
Would you like to write that down? What was that? Can you sketch that? Was that an A.I.? (See Glossary for definition of *Aesthetic Impact, or A.I.)* You mentioned ________. Move to the meaning behind ________ and describe.	Move to the relationship between the _______ and the _______ and describe. Move to the relationship between the _______ you mentioned and the tasked event and describe. Move to the relationship between the vertical object you mentioned and the tasked activity and describe.

During the Remote Viewing session, the use of cueing words or commands will help you get more information and detail about the target site. Our Cue Card is designed to provide you with some ideas. These are only examples. You can be very creative and think of other neutral (not leading!) ways to cue.

Sensory Words

The first list contains Sensory Words. Sensory words relate to your five major senses: taste, touch, smell, hearing, and sight. Start using these words first. Sensory words can be found on the Cue Card at the end of the chapter.

Dimensional Words

Once you have picked up some perceptions that describe the shape, size, pattern, or other dimensional information about the site, you can then begin using the dimensional word list in combination with the sensory word list.

Dimensional words can be found on the Cue Card at the end of the chapter.

Reminders

When using the list of sensory or dimensional words, be sure to read them quickly. Don't give the Viewer (or yourself, if you are self-monitoring) time to answer. These words are only meant to "prod" the subconscious mind.

When working alone, if you ask "Color?" and then stop and think, and then answer, "Blue," you are often answering with your conscious mind. Instead, read the whole list of sensory words to yourself very quickly, and then get back to your viewing. Remember, once you have come up with a dimensional word, both the sensory and dimensional word lists can be used for your word cues.

The same goes for when you are working as the Monitor: Be sure to say the cueing words *too quickly* for the Viewer to answer with his or her conscious mind. If the Viewer begins giving you answers that correspond to the cue, — as in "Color?" "Blue." "Luminance?" "Bright," — you know you are saying the words too slowly. Speed it up, or stop cueing.

Some Advanced and Helpful Cues

Sometimes the Viewer is silent. When the Viewer goes silent, information is lost. A lot is going on in the Viewer's mind that is not getting written down! When this happens, the Monitor can give some advanced cues. Advanced cues, especially when you see changing facial expressions, noises, moving lips, or whispering can be:

"Would you like to write that down?"

"Can you sketch that?"

"What was that?"

"Was that an AI?"

Relationship Cues:

"Move to the relationship between the ______ and the ______ and describe."

Some examples of relationship cues include:

- "Move to the relationship between the water and the manmade and describe."
- "Move to the relationship between the person you mentioned and the tasked event and describe."
- "Move to the relationship between the vertical object you mentioned and the tasked activity and describe."

These are examples. The monitor would create his/her own relationship cues appropriate to the descriptors the Viewer has already perceived.

Whether you are the Monitor, or the Viewer viewing alone, refer to the Cue Card as a guide. It contains a list of cueing words as well as some generic guidance phrases that encourage movement to various parts of the target site or interaction with the target.

10 Attributes of a Good Monitor

1. A good Monitor remains "stone-faced" and physically still during the session, so as not to give anything away about the target or about how the Viewer is doing in session.
2. A good Monitor protects the Viewer. (See: **Protect the Viewer**)
3. A good Monitor puts the needs of the Viewer first and remembers the mantra, "It's all about the Viewer."
4. A good Monitor doesn't move around too much. A fidgety Monitor can be distracting.
5. A good Monitor is curious and wants to know more about the target.
6. A good Monitor asks questions about a perception for clarification purposes, but never leads the Viewer. For example, if the Viewer says "red" and the part of the target you need info on is red, it is okay to say, "Move to the red and describe." But to say, "Is there something red at the target you

can tell me about?" to try to get the Viewer to the red part would be leading, because the Viewer hasn't found the "red" yet.

7. If there are people in the area of the viewing, a good Monitor keeps them quiet, or asks them to leave. Those observing the viewing session must be instructed on remote viewing etiquette to lessen the stress on the Viewer.
8. A good Monitor is sensitive to what is happening with the Viewer.
9. A good Monitor learns when to talk and when to be silent.
10. A good Monitor presents suggestions as questions, rather than orders, as in "Would you like to move to the next page?" instead of "Move to the next page!" or "Would you like a movement command?" rather than interrupting abruptly with "Move to the ______ and describe." *(Refer to **Take Care of the Viewer** for more about Move Commands.)*

Remind the Viewer of the Frontloading or Task

Sometimes the Viewer is on a roll, talking and writing away, clearly making good site contact, but you as the Monitor aren't sure if what the Viewer is describing has anything to do with the tasking.

I sometimes get caught up in describing people at the site. If Jim is not sure how my descriptions relate to the tasking, he will ask, "Move to the relationship between the __________ you are describing and the __________ and describe."

For example, if I am working on a life path for a client, Jim might say, "Move to the relationship between the overbearing male you just described and the life path of the client, and describe."

Often to my own surprise, I quickly explain how the two are connected, which usually opens up an entirely new aspect of the target, revealing important information.

Once I was working on a "Life Path" target for a customer in Europe. This customer wanted to know whether he should consider a possible career or location change, and if so, what change should he make?

During the session, I began describing an overbearing, domineering male. Jim, my Monitor, wanted to keep me on track with the customer's question, and he wondered what this male had to do with the tasking. So, he cued me with, "Move to the relationship between the male you just described and the tasking." I responded with, "This male is going to be a major obstacle in *any* change of career or location, because he is so intent on controlling the client."

The client later said that both the physical description and personality attributes I described matched his boss at work. He left that job and quickly found his niche in a different career entirely.

If the Viewer seems to be drifting away from the main part of the target, you may need to remind the Viewer of the original frontloading.

Examples include:

- "Move back to the Manmade and describe."
- "Move back to the Activity and describe."
- "Move back to the most important part of this Event and describe."

That last one is helpful when the Viewer seems lost: "Move back to the *most important part of this event* and describe." Somehow, the subconscious mind seems to automatically know what is most important, and moves there.

Keep in mind, though, that what is "most important" to *you*, may not necessarily be the most important thing to your subconscious mind, or even to the customer!

In that case, you can suggest to the Viewer: *"Move to what is most important to the customer and describe."*

Joe McMoneagle once mentioned that when conducting a remote viewing target for someone, he asks himself, "Show me what will make the customer happy!" It seems to work well for him.

However, doing what Joe does could get you into trouble, because it could effectively move you *away* from the *tasked* target, to something else that would make the customer happy. It is possible that the *correct* answer to the customer's question won't make him or her happy!

Trust the Viewer

Tension on the part of the Viewer can also be an indication that there is something wrong with the target itself.

I sometimes react to a target that I instinctively know will not be healthy for me to view—seemingly reacting negatively for what appears to be "no reason." But there *is* a reason. The subconscious mind knows what the target is already.

If you, as the Monitor, are blind to the target and the target is operational, it is possible that the customer has chosen a target for a reason other than what he or she indicated to the Project Manager (or to you, if you are acting as both Monitor and Project Manager.)

To clarify, let's say that Project Manager "John Doe" is approached by client "Jane Smith." Jane says she has a project for John Doe's RV team, and that she will pay $5,000 to have them view it. She says it's about her company, Acme Face Cream. She wants to know if a possible new product line will be successful.

But in this example, Jane is actually working for a terrorist organization that is planning a dastardly attack on innocent people, and she wants to know if the *attack* will be successful. She has created a *false scenario* to get information other than what she indicated to the Project Manager. From this example, you can see how a Viewer can inadvertently be used to do something nefarious without even knowing it! But amazingly, I have found that most Viewers can *sense* when they are being tasked with a target they should not view.

After a few unpleasant (but not nefarious) targets that I felt uneasy about, Jim has learned to trust my instincts when it comes to accepting or not accepting certain assignments.

It is the Project Manager's duty to thoroughly vet any potential customer to ensure that the Viewer will not end up being used for a nefarious purpose or anything other than the true goals and intentions represented by the potential customer.

Protect the Viewer

Part of the Monitor's job is to protect the Viewer.

Once I was tasked to find the cause of an airplane crash. The customer already knew that in the aftermath of the crash into the ocean, sharks subsequently attacked some of the survivors.

During the session, I had a visual image in my mind of tigers attacking people. Knowing my Viewer mantra, "Describe, don't identify," I wrote down the "tiger" thoughts and set them aside to the right of my page, and then began mentally eliminating the nouns from my visual impressions. I started describing blood and sounds of tearing flesh. Wanting to protect me and remove me mentally from this carnage, my Monitor simply said, "This is known information. Move back to the Manmade and describe."

There is no reason for a Viewer to subject his or her subconscious mind to information that is unpleasant or potentially harmful—especially when it is of no use to the customer.

In this example, my Monitor did a good job of quickly letting me know that the information I was giving him was not needed before moving me to something else.

The Monitor's job is to protect the Viewer's psyche from unnecessary trauma. There are several ways to circumvent unnecessary trauma for the Viewer. Moving the Viewer around at the target site to something benign can be an effective way to avoid viewing information that is unpleasant and not particularly needed. Another way is to suggest breaks and do something fun in the interim, before going back into session. A very effective method involves the Monitor suggesting that the unpleasant element (such as a dead body) is a cartoon character or, for example, a box of cereal. The Viewer can then safely view the target as the analogous cartoon or benign object while relating what is happening.

For example, let's say that the police have tasked Viewer "Alice" to describe a murder that took place late last Saturday night in a dark alley outside a local bar. Alice, who is blind to the target subject matter, instinctively wants to avoid whatever is happening at the target site. She begins to get nervous and the Monitor realizes she is avoiding the target. She mentions that something bad is happening to a man at the target, but she cannot go any further.

At that point, the Monitor can suggest that the Viewer sees the person as a box of corn flakes. "Alice," says the Monitor, "You said something is happening to a man at the target. Can you imagine for a moment that the man is a box of corn flakes? Tell me what is happening to the box of corn flakes."

Now Alice can safely tell the Monitor, "There are 4 men jumping and slashing the box of corn flakes, and the corn flakes are falling all over the ground," without having the emotional trauma of watching a gruesome murder.

As I've mentioned, some targets can be emotionally damaging to the Viewer, and the Project Manager should know exactly what the goal of the project is and how the target might potentially affect the Viewer.

Here are just a few examples of targets that could be damaging to a Viewer, or that could constitute a ***mis***use of the Viewer to do something that he/she would never knowingly agree to do.

- Plan a terrorist attack
- View future disasters
- Participate in corporate espionage
- Spy on someone, such as a spouse or a partner
- View esoteric, unverifiable targets, like "the end of the world"
- View violent targets with carnage, death, or destruction
- View targets of an illegal nature involving or leading to crime. For example, if the customer is a criminal and wants a Viewer to view something that would assist the criminal with burglary or kidnapping.

The Monitor as Project Manager

Nowadays, we don't often have the luxury of a complete remote viewing team, consisting of Viewers, Monitors, Analysts, Report Writers, Project Managers, etc. Because of this, people on the remote viewing team often have to wear multiple hats. The Monitor is sometimes forced to be the Project Manager, dealing with the customer so that the Viewer doesn't have to. It is vitally important to protect the Viewer from the pollution that is inevitable if the Viewer is dealing directly with the customer.

Intuitive Specialists now offers a Project Management and Operational Viewing course to students that have reached an advanced level of skill and are interested in creating their own remote viewing business or just want to be capable of handling their own incoming projects.

It is the Project Manager's job to screen each potential customer. However, even the best Project Managers have been known to accept targets that end up having negative consequences.

When the viewing session begins, if the Viewer is behaving oddly, in a tense manner, or exhibiting emotional reactions to the target, stop everything, suggest a break, and double check who the customer is, and what he or she is *really* after!

A student once asked, "Would this be a good time to do a quick ideogram on the customer to see what he or she really wants?" The answer is: It can be, ***if*** you have created and practiced well-established ideograms that are useful for this specific purpose, such as "Dishonesty," "Honesty," or "Hidden Agenda," for example.

If you are not trained in CRV, the next paragraph won't mean anything to you. But for the CRVers among you, this shouldn't be unfamiliar:

You can create a column in the Phase or Stage 4 column structure (known as "the P4 Matrix") to find out the customer's *true* motive. Occasionally when viewing, to find out what the customer or tasker is really after, Lyn Buchanan creates a column he refers to as the "Tasker's Intent" column.

Like all columns in the P4 matrix, the Viewer can touch the column heading for information, just as he/she can touch an ideogram and get information. The purpose of this column is to simply "tap into" what the customer (aka: tasker) is truly after.

However, be aware that doing this can move the Viewer away from the intended target, so it must be used cautiously. Only use the "Tasker's Intent" column when you feel there is something wrong or when there is a valid reason to check out your customer's reasons for having this particular target viewed.

Seven Tips for the Monitor:

1. Remember that the Monitor's job is not to get the Viewer to the target!
2. The Monitor's job is to help the Viewer get the information flowing.
3. The Monitor helps when the Viewer gets stuck or when information simply stops flowing by assisting with neutral cues.
4. Keep the Viewer moving around and interacting with the target site.
5. Be sure to observe the Viewer closely and offer help as needed.
6. Remember: "It's all about the Viewer."
7. The Viewer is in charge of the session, but the Monitor acts as a guide—not to the target site itself, necessarily, but to help the Viewer stay on task, to monitor the Viewer's needs and emotions, and to

ensure that the Viewer's experience during the session is safe and productive.

Avoid "The Monitor's Cat"

For those unfamiliar with Controlled Remote Viewing, the word "cat" has a very different meaning in CRV "lingo." *CAT* is an abbreviation of the term "Stray Cat." This term was created by Lyn Buchanan and is an acronym meaning: *Subconscious Transference of Recollections, Anxieties and Yearnings to Consciously Accessible Thought.*" It basically refers to perceptions that bubble up from the Subconscious mind that are immediately transformed into a noun. These momentary images or words can quickly grow into a huge story that has nothing to do with the target. This doesn't just happen with Viewers! Monitors can be guilty of making assumptions about the target and even trying to guess what the target might be. That is a big no-no, and is what we refer to as "The Monitor's Cat."

There has been much debate about whether a monitor should know anything at all about the target when monitoring a Viewer in a real-world, operational project. Here are my two cents:

When a target is being worked "double-blind," it is assumed that neither the Viewer nor the Monitor have any knowledge about the target being viewed. In my 20+ years in this field, I have had the opportunity to participate in many remote viewing projects—as a Viewer, Monitor, Project Manager and Director. The results of sessions conducted involving a ***well-trained monitor*** who has enough knowledge about the target to be able to assist the Viewer ***without polluting him/her*** has consistently provided better results in terms of accuracy and answering the question.

Opponents of my opinion feel that anyone with any knowledge of the target should not be in the room while the viewing is going on. I agree that untrained people, especially customers, should not be in the viewing room while the viewing is going on. But a well-trained Monitor is a different story.

Here is why:

- Remember that this is *REMOTE* Viewing. If Faraday cages were unable to keep remote viewers from knowing what the target was during the military days (and if any "mind-reading" or telepathic overlay is going to occur) neither distance nor time can prevent that from happening. Remote Viewers are limitless in that way. That is why when referring to Controlled Remote Viewing it is often said, "There are no secrets."
- A well-trained Monitor will be focused on the Viewer and the structure of the session, not on the target itself. For that reason, he or she will not be polluting the Viewer.
- In most sessions, including the ones that took place in the military unit, the reason for conducting a remote viewing session is because information is needed and no one has it. So, there are always "unknowns" in every session, which means there is ***always*** a double-blind

element to every session. My students are trained to "go after the unknown." A disciplined, well-trained Viewer can go to the target and get the intended information *in spite of pollution.* A good Viewer should even **practice dealing with pollution** for this very reason! Otherwise, what happens when pollution occurs accidentally? If a child's life is at stake, the delicate Viewer who has never had to deal with pollution will have to just say, "Oh, sorry. Can't do it. I am too polluted. I guess the poor kid is just going to have to die." To me, that is unacceptable!

- So, for all the folks out there who believe every session must be 100% pure and free of any frontloading, and that the Monitor must never have knowledge about anything concerning the target, etc., I say, "FOOEY!"
- In my school, I believe in training Viewer and Monitor teams who are tough, versatile, resilient, and who can view under any circumstances. If Controlled

Remote Viewing is the survival skill I believe it to be, then there is no other option.

- What *can* be damaging, however, is if the Monitor knows absolutely nothing about the target, and begins forming his or her own ideas about what the target must be. It is NOT the Monitor's job to guess what the target is, and a well-trained Monitor would not allow this to occur. But if he/she *does*, and if telepathic overlay occurs, guess what? That's right: The Monitor has just derailed the whole session with incorrect, imaginary information that he/she dreamed up and telepathically passed on to the Viewer!
- To sum it up, if a Monitor has at least minimal knowledge about the target and some telepathic overlay occurs, the Monitor's knowledge will more than likely cause the Viewer to get closer to the target. If a Monitor has zero knowledge about the target, and telepathic overlay occurs, his or her ideas about the target

> will more than likely lead the Viewer *away* from the target. Therefore, once you are well-trained as a Monitor and you are working on professional-level projects, make sure that at the very least, you know what the customer's question is.

That being said, a Monitor who is mostly blind to the target and only has a bit of information can still become a deterrent to a successful session if he/she has opinions or ideas about that target and influences the Viewer accordingly.

Therefore, when you are the Monitor, be sure to allow your Viewer the space to view without your interference or doubts.

You may feel that the Viewer is off target. We have observed many times that when it appears the Viewer is wrong or off target, it turns out that he or she is actually *right* and the information being provided is correct. Again, it is important to *trust the Viewer.*

Being the Monitor or Project Manager who has to send in the final report to a paying customer can feel like a big responsibility. But remember that you are not the Viewer, so you must trust that what you send will be correct. And if it is not correct, it will be a good learning experience.

Ultimately, while we hope it would be the rare exception, you can always refund the customer's money or offer to do another session.

Castle Building

A student once asked, "What do you do when the Viewer really *is* off target and has gone off on a tangent and is building a big mental castle?" (*Find more about Castle Building in **Appendix B**.)*

The answer: Ignore it.

Remember: The Viewer is in charge of the session.

As mentioned earlier, it could be that you are mistaken. And if you are not mistaken, it can be that the Viewer is taking time to "get on target."

If the Viewer senses your nervousness, he or she will feel off target. This will only worsen the situation and lower the Viewer's confidence.

As a Viewer, I am sometimes "off target" for as many as ten pages! But Jim has learned over time that this is my way of creating a "warm up" period. So nowadays, he simply relaxes and lets me work. Then I get on target.

A student once asked, "But if the Viewer has a big castle going, and *knows* it, how do I get them out of the castle and back to viewing the target?"

Ask the Viewer to write the entire castle out on the right side of the page. Sometimes, just declaring the castle helps to get rid of it.

Another technique I learned from Mel Riley is to have the Viewer ask him or herself:

- What about this castle is similar to the target?
- What about this castle is not like the target?

While this method might be considered "viewing a stray cat," it can help the Viewer extrapolate the ***message*** from the subconscious mind that is being ***represented*** by the castle. Every castle and every stray cat has a grain of truth or a message in it. By viewing the similarities and dissimilarities to the target, the Viewer can evaporate the castle. This is a Phase or Stage 5 tool we use for "blowing out the pipes" and causes a castle or a strong stray cat to dissolve.

You can also say, "Move to that which you ***perceive*** to be a _____ and describe." That way, you are not moving them to the actual stray cat or castle, but by using the words "what you *perceive to be...*" you are reminding the Viewer that the noun he or she has in mind may not be what is really at the target. This allows the Viewer to move to whatever made him/her think there was a "castle" there, and he/she will often discover truths about a part of the target that will dissolve the castle completely.

Detoxing

Hopefully, you already know how to detox. If not, be sure to read our mini class on Detoxing, or, if you haven't already done so, take our CRV course to learn more.

Whether we want to believe it or not, the Monitor often "travels" with the Viewer. Therefore, it is just as important for the Monitor to detox as it is for the Viewer!

To clarify, the Monitor should *never* attempt to view, to become the Viewer, or take over the Viewer's role.

However, a good Monitor sometimes (whether intentionally or unintentionally) "rides along" with the Viewer's mind in order to help the Viewer and keep the Viewer safe. This will inevitably lead to the Monitor sharing the Viewer's reactions and some of the Viewer's experiences at the target site.

Viewers and Monitors who frequently work

together find they easily connect mentally when the Viewer is viewing a target.

It makes sense. Just as husbands and wives often finish each other's sentences or find they are thinking the same thought at the same time, Viewers and Monitors get to know each other very well through the process of viewing and monitoring.

As a Monitor, be sure to pay attention to everything the Viewer is saying. Once, when I was working on a kidnapping case, I found myself communicating to the subconscious mind of a guard who was guarding the victim. As I connected to this person, I came to understand the ideology of the group—their "cause," so to speak—and suddenly I looked up and said, "We may be helping the wrong side!" Jim blinked calmly and asked softly, "Does someone need to detox?"

That's right: I found myself *sympathizing* with the kidnappers! How can something like this happen? The Viewer is linking to the subconscious mind of another person, and this can allow the Viewer to really see the world or situation *as the person being viewed sees it.*

Viewers come out of sessions understanding why the murderer killed his victim, why the rapist raped the child, etc., as horrific as such acts are. As Lyn Buchanan frequently says, "CRV is not a toy. It is the real thing."

For this reason, detoxing is imperative. To learn more about how to detox from any situation, remote viewing session, or psychic influences, read the section on Detoxing in my upcoming book, *"Boundless: Your How-To Guide to* ***Practical*** *Remote Viewing!"*

ERV Monitoring

Just as I thought I was done with this book, I had a conversation with my good friend, Mel Riley. Mel was the very first soldier to become a part of what was, at the time, the newly created military psychic spying unit. He also has the distinction of being the only member of the unit to have served two separate tours of duty as a Viewer in the unit.

Mel asked me if I intended to include a section on "ERV Monitoring." For those of you who are not familiar with it, ERV, or Extended Remote Viewing, is a form of remote viewing in which the Viewer is in a hypnogogic state while viewing. I'll explain.

During the 20-year history of the unit, a lot of experimentation was done and "remote viewing" went through a lot of incarnations. ERV experiments were conducted differently by the various unit directors as they came and went.

The methodology that intrigued me the most was an Extended Remote Viewing (ERV) technique in which the Viewer would lie down, with the Monitor in a chair nearby. The Monitor would talk the Viewer into a relaxed state and then skillfully guide the Viewer to and around the Target site.

As a former hypnotherapist, I recognize hypnosis when I see it. If you were to ask me how to be a good ERV Monitor, I would suggest that you find a reputable hypnosis school and become certified as a hypnotherapist before attempting to act as a Monitor for an ERV'er.

In my *Beyond Advanced: CRV for Professional Viewers* course, Advanced Viewers gather to spend a few days accessing their individual targets using CRV before attempting to access the target via ERV. Each time a Viewer accesses a target, that particular target becomes easier to view. The act of viewing the target repeatedly builds a sort of "memory path" to the target.

If you have ever gone hiking in a remote, thickly forested area, you know what it is like to hack through uncharted territory. Difficult! But the more people that use a path, the easier it becomes to walk that path, right? It is the same thing with consciousness. We are all linked on some level, so the more people that view a target, the easier that target becomes to view *for everyone.*

I once heard a story about an experiment in which a group of Americans with no knowledge of Mandarin (a Chinese language) were divided into two groups of 500 people. Group A was given a recording of a famous Chinese lullaby and asked to mimic the sounds and memorize it. Group B was given the same lullaby, but the words were scrambled up. Since neither group understood the language anyway, it shouldn't have made any difference. Both groups were trying to memorize a group of what were, to them, meaningless sounds in a melody.

Interestingly, Group A (the group with the version of the lullaby that over a billion Chinese people know) learned the song 20 times faster than Group B. This would indicate that when a lot of people know something, it becomes easier to learn. Why? Because the knowledge is "out there" in the ethers, and we are all connected.

So, when a Viewer is able to repeatedly view the same target, it becomes easier to view. After two or three days of viewing that target, the Viewer is ready to relax into a comfortable recliner and allow the soft, controlled voice of the Monitor to lull him/her into a relaxed state.

In that state, the Viewer easily accesses the target, which he/she is already familiar with due to the CRV sessions already performed. A skilled Monitor is able to gently guide the Viewer (without "leading") to the target and then have the Viewer move to various parts of the site, giving information about each aspect while remaining in that perfect hypnogogic state.

There are many levels of consciousness. With experience, the ERV Monitor helps the Viewer move up and down through as many as 40 levels of consciousness, interviewing the Viewer all the while. It is important for the session to be recorded and transcribed so that the information is not lost.

Because this type of ERV requires so much skill on the part of the Monitor (and cannot, in fact, be done *without* a Monitor), there are not many teachers who can correctly teach this method. In lieu of that, some teachers will have their students sit in chairs or lie on the floor under a blanket, and simply ask them to "access the target." Then, after a set amount of time has passed, the students are roused and asked to write down what they "saw" or what they experienced.

The drawback to doing ERV this way is that so much information is lost because the students remember so little of what they experienced during the time they were, essentially, napping.

With both CRV and ERV, the information should be captured *as it is being experienced.* In CRV, the Viewer is writing everything down as perceptions are coming in. With the type of ERV I prefer, the one that uses a Monitor trained in hypnosis, the entire session is recorded using a digital recording device so that no information will be lost.

The Monitor simply needs to make sure that both the Monitor and Viewer have a lapel microphone or something similar that will pick up even the quietest whispers. (Note: Viewers often begin speaking very softly when in that state. It can be hard to pick up those sounds unless there is a microphone right by the Viewer's lips.)

Ultimately, it is probably best not to attempt to monitor for ERV sessions unless you have been trained in hypnosis and are experienced as a Controlled Remote Viewer yourself.

Conclusion

If you have no experience as a Monitor and that makes you feel uneasy—don't fret! Jump in and give monitoring a try. You'll enjoy it, and you'll find that *being* monitored is great, too!

As you practice both monitoring and being monitored, your skills in many areas will greatly improve. And as they improve, viewing becomes more fascinating than you ever imagined!

Thank you for reading this guide, and may it be a terrific and oft-used reference tool as you and your viewing partner(s) forge ahead in the exploration of the newest frontier: Consciousness!

We announce special offers and upcoming courses in our newsletter, so be sure to sign up to receive it!

We enjoy hearing from our students and readers!

Contact us at:

Lori & Jim Williams
Email: **info@IntuitiveSpecialists.com**
Web: http://intuitivespecialists.com

Workshops Offered by Intuitive Specialists

For a complete list of our **remote viewing courses** and detailed descriptions, please visit our **website**, intuitivespecialists.com

Controlled Remote Viewing—Level One Basic

Controlled Remote Viewing—Level Two Intermediate

Controlled Remote Viewing—Level Three Advanced

Beyond Advanced: CRV for Professional Viewers

Health and Healing Applications for Remote Viewers

Associative Remote Viewing

Extended Remote Viewing

Appendix A: How to Monitor Online

Many Viewers use Skype, GoToMeeting, or a similar program to monitor each other. For online monitoring, it is helpful if the Viewer has a webcam that is adjustable. Some webcams, especially those made for a PC, are like Cyclops heads on little necks, and you can adjust them as needed. When that is the case, you can position the camera so it allows the Monitor to see the Viewer's head and upper body.

If that is *not* the case, the Viewer may have to move back, away from the screen. In our home, the camera is built into the top of our monitor, and there is very little mobility. The monitor can be tipped downward, but it doesn't move very far. So, if I were going to be monitored online, I would need to bring a small table to sit farther back from the computer.

However, if the Viewer sits too far from the computer, the Monitor may not be able to see the Viewer's eye movements or facial expressions, which is very important. You and your CRV Buddy may have to decide what works best based on trial and error.

You can also use a dual-webcam setup, which allows the Monitor to see the Viewer's face and upper body, while at the same time observing the Viewer's hand and the paper. YouTube has several good videos about how to do this.

During our online classes, students have been able to use their desktop or laptop camera for the face and upper body. Then, signing in to Skype or GoToMeeting on a separate device (smart phone or tablet, for example) they can use that device's camera to show the paper on the table. It takes some maneuvering to get the second camera positioned just right to clearly see the paper and pen of the Viewer, but once positioned, it works great.

Appendix B: Terms Used in This Book

The terms listed below are not in alphabetical order. Instead, they are in the order that they appear in the book or in order of their importance to the process. If you are not a Controlled Remote Viewer, and are unfamiliar with the terms in this book, you should read this section first.

Source

This is the unknowable source of information. Some people feel that the information gained from a remote viewing session comes from the Akashic Records, God, Angels, Guides, the "great big Cosmic Database in the Sky," etc. Whatever you believe, this publication simply refers to the source of the information as the subconscious mind and in some cases as "The Source."

Controlled Remote Viewing (CRV)

CRV is the structured process that was developed by Ingo Swann, known by some as "the father of remote viewing," after the U.S. military hired him to help them devise a method for turning soldiers into "psychic spies." This method utilizes the functions of the left and right sides of the brain, along with other techniques that are designed to allow the conscious and subconscious minds of the Remote Viewer to communicate with each other. CRV is comparable to a drawer organizer for that pesky junk drawer we all have. The structure itself allows a Viewer to categorize his or her thoughts based on what part of the brain the thoughts are originating from, effectively separating true psychic perceptions from imagination, for example.

Remote Viewer (RV'er, Viewer)

A Remote Viewer has learned techniques that allow him or her to access information via an intuitive process. As currently understood, the subconscious mind has access to all information, to everything in all of time and space, and to everything that has ever happened, is happening, or that will happen. Sometimes, this information is inaccessible through normal means—for example, when a crime is committed for which there are no witnesses. A Remote Viewer can access that information using remote viewing.

Controlled Remote Viewer, or CRV'er

A Controlled Remote Viewer is someone who has been trained in the structured protocols of CRV, a method developed by Ingo Swann.

Monitor

The Monitor is a person who assists the Viewer. A Remote Viewer can have a much more accurate and successful remote viewing session when a trained Monitor sits with him or her and helps the Viewer stay within the structured CRV protocol. Neutral "cues" can also be given to prompt the Viewer to get more information.

Tasker

A Tasker is the person who is seeking information. The Tasker is usually the customer, friend, or person who requested a remote viewing session.

CRV Buddy

A CRV Buddy is a Remote Viewer who is paired with another Remote Viewer to practice together as a Viewer-Monitor team on a regular basis.

Stray Cat

Stray Cat is an acronym developed by Lyn Buchanan. It stands for *Subconscious Transference of Recollections, Anxieties, and Yearnings to Consciously Accessible Thought.* Ingo Swann used the term "AOL" or "Analytic Overlay" rather than Stray Cat. However, Analytic Overlay comes from the logical, conscious mind. A Stray Cat comes from the subconscious mind. Current-day Viewers sometimes use the two terms interchangeably. Usually a noun, a Stray Cat identifies, rather than describes. The Viewer perceives "orange, round, rubbery" and immediately thinks of a basketball. The word "basketball" would be a Stray Cat or an AOL. When a Stray Cat arises from the subconscious mind, it often comes up as a memory, a fear, or a desire. The Viewer suddenly remembers playing basketball as a kid with his dad, for example, which leads to the idea that there is a basketball at the target. Stray Cats and AOL's are not necessarily wrong—they can be correct—but they are more often symbolic or carry messages about the target, rather than being the target itself.

Cat

This is the short name for Stray Cat. It is the generic name for any of several types of impressions that result from the output of the conscious mind, rather than from the subconscious mind, or from the "true source" of incoming information. Examples are: Anxiety Cat, Memory Cat, the Tasker's (or Customer's) Cat, and as mentioned below, the Monitor's Cat.

Castle Building

This is another Lyn Buchanan term, used to describe a situation in which a Remote Viewer has perceived something accurate about the target, but then digresses because he or she has linked the correct perception to an incorrect situation. For example, a Viewer is doing a practice target. The photo in the envelope is of an aqueduct built on tall white pillars. The Viewer perceives "tall, white, vertical, parallel, cylindrical" for the pillars, but then immediately assumes these cylindrical objects are the goal posts in a soccer game. Then the Viewer starts describing the game, the players, and the uniforms. He has "built a castle" based on his assumption that the pillars are goal posts.

Gestalt

The term "Gestalt," used in the context of a CRV session, means "overall concept" or a generalized idea.

Ideogram

Ideagrams are symbols that represent gestaltic words, ideas or concepts. Viewers can develop an ever-growing list of gestaltic words and accompanying Ideogrammic symbols to utilize in the beginning stages of a CRV session. These symbols are initially taught to the subconscious mind, just as your subconscious mind has learned the way to your house. Have you ever driven home deep in thought, pulled in your driveway, and realized you were unaware of the drive? Your subconscious mind was controlling your body while your conscious mind daydreamed away. In the same way, the subconscious mind can be taught a series of symbols that represent certain concepts, allowing the Viewer to create the symbols in a subconscious "scribble" that can be deciphered to give information. (Check out our FREE Ideogram Practice at intuitivespecialists.com.)

Target

Whatever is chosen for a Remote Viewer to examine via remote viewing is known as a Target. This can be anything at all in the whole of time and space. It can include objects, people, locations, activities, and events—to name a few. The Target can be in the past, present, or future—or all three. Even concepts can be viewed. Once a session is complete, the Viewer can sometimes receive feedback. When feedback is unavailable and will perhaps never be available in the Viewer's lifetime, the target is considered to be an *esoteric* target. If there is provable feedback, the target is considered a *hard* target.

Frontloading

Often the Viewer receives no information about the target prior to the viewing. However, we have found that it can be beneficial to give the Viewer some broad and neutral information beforehand, as it helps the Viewer become accustomed to pollution. This neutral information is known as *frontloading*. The decision as to whether any particular session is frontloaded beforehand is always the Viewer's. The Monitor is never to force the Viewer to accept frontloading.

A Few Examples of Neutral Frontloading:

The Target is manmade. Describe the Target.

The Target is a location. Describe the Target.

The Target is biological. Describe the Target.

The Target is an activity. Describe the Target.

The Target is a person. Describe the Target.

Examples of *Advanced* Frontloading:

(The following examples would be for less common Targets and the frontloading that can be given to a Viewer as the session begins.)

The Target is a Journey. Describe the Target.

The Target is a Process. Describe the Target.

The Target is a Life Path. Describe the Target.

The Target is a Technology. Describe the Target.

The Target is a Society. Describe the Target.

Appendix C: Helpful Forms

The forms in Appendix C are here for you to copy and use in your intuitive teamwork, especially for those in Controlled Remote Viewing teams.

The Monitor's Worksheet

V #:	Viewer's Name:	Monitor's Name:

Date:	Target Coordinate:	Frontloading Given (if any):

Break Times:	Resume Times:	List Any Observers:	Gestalts to Cue From:

Track Page Numbers with Tic Marks Here:

Micromovements:	Perceptions to Explore Further:

Notes	Page #'s to Remember:

Monitor's Cue Card

SENSORY WORDS:	DIMENSIONAL WORDS:
Colors? Illumination? Textures? Density? Temperature? Smells? Tastes? Sounds? Ambience?	Shapes? Sizes? Patterns? Positions? Direction? Orientation?
ACTION CUE EXAMPLES:	**MOVEMENT COMMAND EXAMPLES:**
Mentally lick the target. Taste? Mentally slap the target. Density? Clap your hands at the target. Sounds?	Move 10 feet back from the target and describe. Move 50 feet above the target and describe. Move 2 minutes forward and describe. Move underneath the target and describe. Move 12 hours forward and describe what you see. Turn 180° degrees at the target and describe.
OCCASIONAL QUESTIONS:	**ADVANCED CUES:**
Would you like to write that down? What was that? Can you sketch that? Was that an A.I.? (See Glossary for definition of *Aesthetic Impact, or A.I.)* You mentioned ________. Move to the meaning behind ________ and describe.	Move to the relationship between the _______ and the _______ and describe. Move to the relationship between the _______ you mentioned and the tasked event and describe. Move to the relationship between the vertical object you mentioned and the tasked activity and describe.

Appendix D: Quick Guides

These are guides to the Administration Section and the first three Phases of the Controlled Remote Viewing Structure. I have included them in Appendix D for Monitors who may be untrained in the CRV structure.

By having this information at your fingertips, you will be better equipped to assist the Remote Viewer.

Quick Guide to: The Administrative Section of the CRV Session

The Administrative section of your CRV session is the first thing that goes on your paper. You write it in the **upper right-hand section** on the first page of your session.

NAME: First, write your name. You can use both your first and last name. Or, if you prefer or need anonymity, you can use your viewer number instead of writing your name.

DATE: Write the date any way you want.

STARTING TIME: Traditionally, as CRV was created for the military, military time is used throughout the session. So, for example, 1:15 p.m. would be 13:15 hrs. (Just add 12 to any time after noon.)

YOUR WORKING LOCATION: Include conditions, such as "I just ate lunch," or, "I just worked out." This will help you establish a pattern. After doing 40 or 50 sessions, you can look back and see that you do your best work, for example, after a jog, or that you can't view your way out of a paper bag if you are trying to view right after a heavy meal.

MONITOR'S NAME: If you do not have a monitor, write "NM" for no monitor.

OBSERVERS: If you are working alone, you can just write "Alone."

POCA'S: Previews of Coming Attractors. This is where you put down the things that jump into your mind, like "Taj Mahal" right before you start your session. It may be a visual thing, or an audible thing, or just a thought. For whatever reason, you think you know what the target is.

POCD'S: Previews of Coming Distractors. This is where you write down things you think will bother you while you are in session. Things like, "Did I pay the gas bill?" or, "I told Susan to call me in 15 minutes," or, "I had a fight with my best friend yesterday." You can abbreviate these by writing "Gas Bill" or "Phone Call" or "Fight."

SET ASIDES: Remember, here is where you MUST set all of your POCA's and POCD's aside. It is so important to do this step properly.

First, state the problem. Then, talk to yourself about it, and why it doesn't have to be a problem right now. You can make a bargain or an agreement with your sub-conscious mind that if it will allow you to set this aside while you are doing your session, you will pick it back up after the session and deal with the problem then.

Second, say the pat phrase: "So for now, I am not worrying about it."

Third, say "For now, I am setting aside ___________." And write it as you say it.

CRV: PHASE ONE TEMPLATE

Use this template as a guide. It will help remind you of the CRV structure for Phase One.

Name:
Date:
Time:
Location:
Circumstances
Monitor:
Observers:
P.O.C.A.:
P.O.C.D.:
S.A.

Coordinates & Ideogram

A: Motion Feeling
B: Gestalt (AKA: Wild-Assed Guess or WAG)

(Ask yourself, "There may be more gestalts at the site. Would you like to take the coordinates

again?" Then continue taking the coordinates, doing the ideogram, the A (motion and feeling) and then the B (Gestalt or WAG) until you feel that you want to move into Phase Two.)

Coordinates & Ideogram

A: Motion Feeling
B: Gestalt (AKA: Wild-Assed Guess or WAG)

PHASE TWO TEMPLATE

This template will serve as a guide to you once you are ready to move into Phase Two. There are three reasons to move from Phase One to Phase Two: You've taken the coordinates several times, and the gestalts keep repeating themselves. For example, you get "Land," "Water," "Manmade," "Land," Water," "Manmade." That is an indicator that you are ready to move into Phase Two.

Another indicator might be when you touch the ideogram for a tactile sensation and you get a sensory descriptor instead. Phase Two descriptors are beginning to "bleed" into your Phase One work. That's an indicator that you are ready to move into Phase Two. Lastly, you've taken the coordinates several times and you just **decide** to move into Phase Two. You are the Viewer. You are in charge.

This template is only an example of what you might get in Phase Two. You label the top left of the page "P2" to show that you are moving into Phase Two. Then, in parenthesis, put one of your "B's." That is to say, put the gestalt that you are going to focus on. Remember that at this point, you are "winking about the site." The descriptors you get after you have chosen the gestalt you are going to focus on may describe other gestalts, too. At this point in the session, your subconscious mind is all over the place, describing this and that.

P2 (Manmade)
Brown
Red
Shiny
Blue
Flat
Reflective
Glossy

(Move up 20 feet and describe)

Square
Multiple
Rectangular
Structural
Intermittent

Remember that you (or your Monitor) can use many types of "cues" to help yourself get more information about the target. Cue yourself with the list of Sensory and Dimensional Cues, Action Cues or Movement Cues, which can be found on the "Cue Card" Template. Be sure to write down any cues that begin with the magic word "MOVE." Writing down where you are moving at the target site is very important for post-session analysis. That way, you'll always know that the perceptions you've gotten once you have moved are perceptions from a different part of the site, and are not the same thing you were describing before.

Tangy tasting
Salty tasting
Tall
Ocean smell

Stray Cat: Ocean scene

PHASE THREE TEMPLATE

Phase Three is sketching/graphics. You don't have to be an artist to use Phase Three effectively. The idea is that you are allowing your subconscious mind to communicate to your conscious mind through your body by putting lines on the paper.

Some Viewers are amazing artists. Others cannot even draw a stick figure. Either way, Phase Three can be extremely useful. Whether it clears the Viewer's mind, or presents information that can be crucial in an operational viewing, Phase Three will become one of the Viewer's favorites.

Here are some basics for the Viewer to remember about Phase Three:

- If you draw something that doesn't feel right, simply cross out that sketch and make a new one. Avoid correcting a sketch on top of a sketch.
- Remember that your sketches are ideograms. You can touch them and get information from them.

- The blank areas around your sketch are full of information about the target. As you touch the sketch and the areas around it, you can pick up information about the target. When that happens, put a number at that location on the paper. On another piece of paper, write down the number as a reference and list the information you found. You can "cross reference" each page so that anyone who looks at your session will understand what you found on the sketch page.
- Remember that the subconscious mind sees with the eyes of a child. Your drawings will enlarge what the subconscious feels is "important." Other parts may be minimized.

Legal Caveat

The information in this or any publication presented by LWE, LLC is not intended to represent or replace advice from a qualified physician or professional consultant in any field of expertise.

Students are advised not to attempt to diagnose or treat disease or illness unless they have the appropriate medical credentials.

Where and when appropriate, any skills learned from this or any other course offered by Intuitive Specialists are intended to be utilized in cooperation with a qualified medical or other appropriate professional.

For permission requests, questions, comments, or any other communication with Intuitive Specialists, email us at:

Info@IntuitiveSpecialists.com

Made in United States
North Haven, CT
03 February 2024

48279245R10072